No M

Written and Illustrated by Esther Smith

This book is dedicated to: my boys
for inspiring me to write this.

ISBN 978-1-59433-287-6

Library of Congress Catalog Card Number:
2012933251

Book designed by Esther Smith

For additional copies of No More Diaper please visit:
http://www.esthersmithbooks.com

Publication Consultants
http://www.publicationconsultants.com

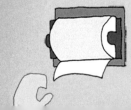

Here is me in my diaper!

I went poopy and potty in my diaper!

"No! No! No! Yucky!" mommy says.

"No more diaper!
No more poopy
and potty
in your diaper!

You are
a big boy now...

Big boys go potty on the toilet!"

Mommy says,
"Only babies wear diapers,"

But I want to be a baby ...
So, why can't I wear a diaper?

I want to be a baby ... because when I was a baby my mommy and daddy spent more time with me.

They hugged and kissed me all the time...
but as I get bigger they don't hug, kiss and hold me as much any more.

Does that mean ...
that they love me less?

I am sad
because I feel like
if I get any
bigger... or do "big
boy" things - like
going potty
on the toilet -
they won't love me
like they used to.

Mommy tells me that she will be so
proud of me - and happy,
if I go poopy on the toilet ...

But she used to be
proud of me
when I went
poo poo
or potty
in my diaper.

I am so
confused!

I guess the only way to find out if mommy
will be happy or mad - is to try it
and see what happens.

So, here goes...

First thing to do is:
Pull down your pants and underwear.

Next is to:
put your soft potty seat on the toilet, and step onto your stool.

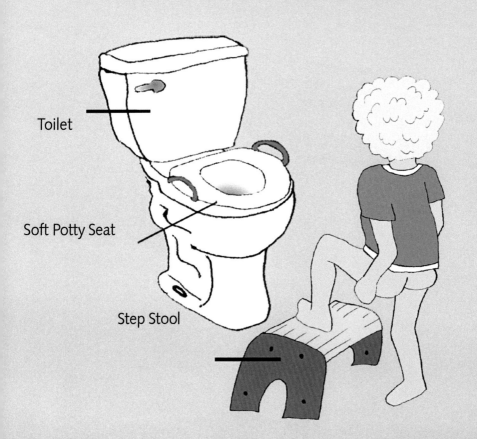

Toilet

Soft Potty Seat

Step Stool

Then: sit down on the toilet
if you have to go poo,

or stand like this, if you have to pee.

And now: you wait!
You can read a book, sing a song, or just be
very still. Just sit or stand and wait and wait
until your body goes.

When: you feel
your body
getting tense and wiggly
- because you have potty
or poopy inside you -
Then: relax and let it
come out of you and
into the toilet.

When you need to go poopy:
you push hard like this,
and you make the
poo poo into the toilet.

Wow! You did it!

The hard part
is over.
Now, take some
toilet paper
and wipe your
bottom clean.

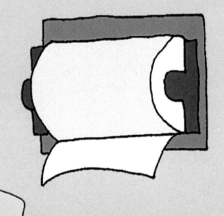

Wipe the back.

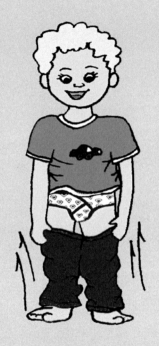

Now, pull up your underwear and your pants.

Now that the toilet is full of poopy and potty...

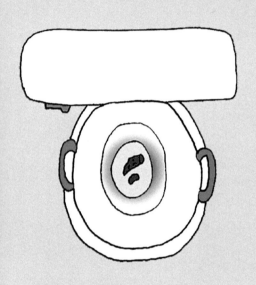

push
down

Flush the toilet, by pushing
the lever down - and watch the
poo poo and pee pee disappear.

And, last of all...
wash and dry your hands.

Now:
Let's see mommy and daddy's faces.

Will they still seem upset,
mad and frustrated?

Or... will they be happy and
proud of me - like they said
that they would be.

I see them. They are happy!

"Yay!!! Good boy!"
They say... "You are so big now.
You went potty and poopy on the toilet.
We are so proud of you!"

Then something crazy happened...

Mommy's happy face suddenly had tears of
water running down her cheeks.

I asked my mommy why she was sad - and mommy told me something very special.

"I am not sad," she said. "I am so happy ...that I am crying. These are called tears of joy. People only cry these 'happy tears' ... when they are happier than they have ever been before, and when they love somebody more today than they did yesterday."

"You mean you love me more right now, than when I was a baby?" I asked my mommy.

or

"Of course I do," she told me.
"Each day I love you more than the day before - because I learn more about what you like, who you are, and the things you can do now - than I knew about you yesterday".

"I am so proud that you have been brave enough to go poopy and potty on the toilet" she said.

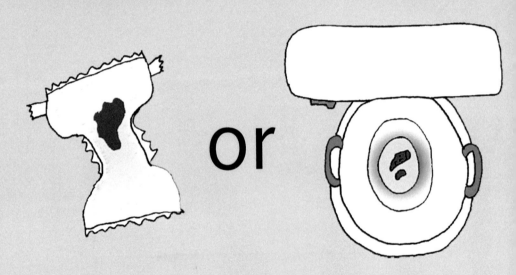

"I know that it is scary, and that it is very different from what you are used to ... But different can be a very wonderful thing".

Mommy says, "I hold and hug you differently than when you were a baby, NOT because I love you any less. It is because your body is growing and changing to be more like daddy's, and now you are getting too big to be held like a baby. Grandpa and mommy love daddy and they don't carry him around".

"There are different phases and stages of love and life. They are not based on age and no one can push you into them. You have been in stage #2 for a while now, but you are finally graduating into stage #3. I am so happy and love you so much!"

Now I know:
that going potty and poopy in the toilet is not only a good thing ... but it is wonderful! Mommy loves me more today than yesterday, and she is so happy - that even her eyes made water!

No More Baby Me

No More Diaper